Vehicle-Mania!

Auto-Mania!

By David Kimber

Gareth Stevens Publishing
A WORLD ALMANAC EDUCATION GROUP COMPANY

Please visit our web site at: www.garethstevens.com
For a free color catalog describing Gareth Stevens Publishing's list
of high-quality books and multimedia programs, call 1-800-542-2595 (USA)
or 1-800-387-3178 (Canada). Gareth Stevens Publishing's fax: (414) 332-3567.

Library of Congress Cataloging-in-Publication Data

Kimber, David, 1960–
    Auto-mania! / by David Kimber. — North American ed.
        p. cm. — (Vehicle-mania!)
    Includes index.
    Contents: Aston Martin V12 Vanquish — BMW Z8 — Bugatti EB 110 — Chevrolet Corvette Z06 —
Dodge Viper GTS — Ferrari F50 — Jaguar XJ220S — Lamborghini Murciélago — McLaren F1—
Mercedes-Benz SL500 — Pagani Zonda C12S — Porsche 911 GT2 — TVR Tuscan.
    ISBN 0-8368-3781-9 (lib. bdg.)
    1. Sports cars—Juvenile literature. [1. Sports cars. 2. Automobiles.] I. Title. II. Series.
TL236.K56 2003
629.222'1—dc21
                                                                    2003043921

This North American edition first published in 2004 by
Gareth Stevens Publishing
A WRC Media Company
330 West Olive Street, Suite 100
Milwaukee, Wisconsin 53212

This U.S. edition copyright © 2004 by Gareth Stevens Inc. Original edition copyright © 2003 ticktock Entertainment Ltd.
First published in Great Britain in 2003 by ticktock Media Ltd., Unit 2, Orchard Business Centre, North Farm Road,
Tunbridge Wells, Kent, TN2 3XF, United Kingdom.

We would like to thank: Tim Bones, Chris Lowe of *Fast Cars* magazine, and Elizabeth Wiggans.

Gareth Stevens Editor: Jim Mezzanotte
Gareth Stevens Art Direction: Tammy West

Photo credits: all the pictures are from the Car Photo Library, www.carphoto.co.uk.

Printed in the United States of America

2 3 4 5 6 7 8 9 09 08 07 06 05

CONTENTS

ASTON MARTIN V12 VANQUISH

The British car company Aston Martin made its first sports car in 1914. Since then, the company has become famous for its high-performance cars. The V12 Vanquish was first sold in 2001. With a powerful **V12 engine** and a lightweight **aluminum** body, it is one of the fastest cars in the world.

Did You Know?

In the movie *Die Another Day*, superspy James Bond drives a V12 Vanquish.

The V12 Vanquish has tire pressure **sensors**, rain sensors, and even sensors that turn on the headlights when it gets dark!

The V12 Vanquish has special paddles behind the steering wheel for shifting gears. The paddles let a driver shift while still holding the wheel.

FACTS AND STATS

First Model Year: 2001

Origin: Britain

Weight:
4,046 pounds
(1,835 kilograms)

Engine:
5,935 cubic centimeter (cc)
V12, front-mounted

Maximum Power:
460 **horsepower** (hp)

Acceleration:
0 to 60 miles
(0 to 97 kilometers)
per hour in 4.5 seconds

Maximum Speed:
190 miles (306 km) per hour

The body panels of the V12 Vanquish are shaped by hand so they fit together perfectly.

BMW Z8

The BMW Z8 is a modern sports car with **retro** looks. The car has a body style based on the BMW 507, a sports car from the 1950s. Thanks to a powerful **V8 engine,** the Z8 is fast as well as beautiful. Without an electronic speed reducer, its top speed would be 180 miles (290 km) per hour.

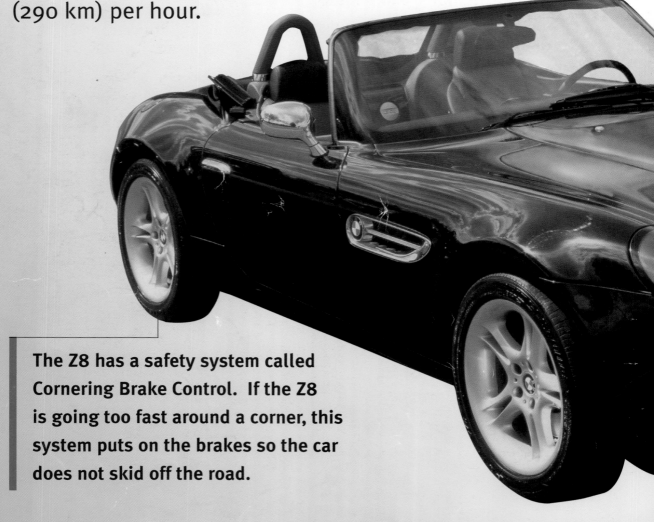

The Z8 has a safety system called Cornering Brake Control. If the Z8 is going too fast around a corner, this system puts on the brakes so the car does not skid off the road.

The Z8 has dials in the center of the dashboard instead of behind the steering wheel.

The Z8 is a **convertible**. It has a soft top that can be raised or lowered at the touch of a button.

Did You Know?

The Z8 has a **satellite navigation system** hidden in the dashboard.

BUGATTI EB 110

In the 1920s and 1930s, Ettore Bugatti made some of the most successful racing cars in the world. Bugatti died in 1947, and his company eventually went out of business. In 1991, a French company began making a new car with the Bugatti name — the fast and beautiful EB 110.

"EB" stands for Ettore Bugatti, who would have been 110 years old when the car was first built.

The body of the EB 110 is made of **carbon fiber.** Unlike most cars, the EB 110 has doors that swing upward.

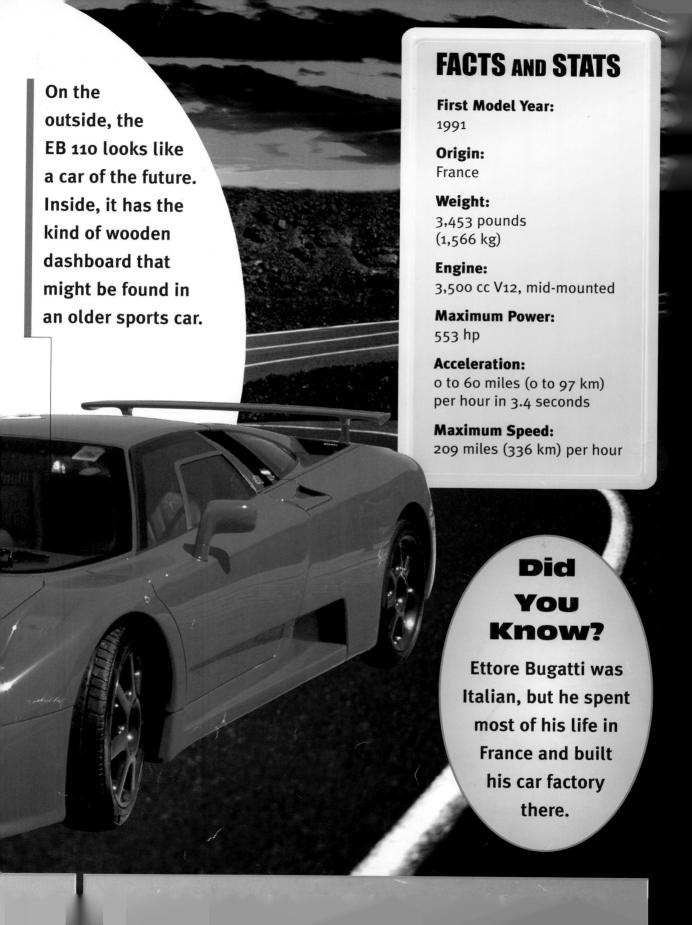

On the outside, the EB 110 looks like a car of the future. Inside, it has the kind of wooden dashboard that might be found in an older sports car.

FACTS AND STATS

First Model Year:
1991

Origin:
France

Weight:
3,453 pounds
(1,566 kg)

Engine:
3,500 cc V12, mid-mounted

Maximum Power:
553 hp

Acceleration:
0 to 60 miles (0 to 97 km) per hour in 3.4 seconds

Maximum Speed:
209 miles (336 km) per hour

Did You Know?

Ettore Bugatti was Italian, but he spent most of his life in France and built his car factory there.

CHEVROLET CORVETTE Z06

Chevrolet built the first Corvette in 1953, and it soon became one of the world's most popular sports cars. Over the years, millions of Corvettes have been sold. The latest model is called the Zo6. Like all Corvettes, the Zo6 has a **fiberglass** body and a powerful engine. It is a fun, fast car at a reasonable price.

Did You Know?

Over 200 of the earliest Corvettes have survived. They are now highly collectible.

Since 1999, the Corvette has had an unusual feature. The car's speed, rpm, and fuel level are projected onto the windshield!

The 1960 Corvette had a top speed of 130 miles (209 km) per hour. At the time, most cars had a top speed under 100 miles (161 km) per hour.

FACTS AND STATS

First Model Year:
1997

Origin:
United States

Weight:
3,116 pounds
(1,413 kg)

Engine:
5,666 cc V8, front-mounted

Maximum Power:
385 hp

Acceleration:
0 to 60 miles (0 to 97 km)
per hour in 4 seconds

Maximum Speed:
175 miles (282 km) per hour

The Corvette comes in three body styles. The coupe has a hard top that cannot be removed. The targa (above) has a roof panel that can be lifted out. The convertible has a folding top.

DODGE VIPER GTS

In the 1960s, Carol Shelby created a sports car called the Shelby Cobra. Many years later, he helped create another car named after a snake — the Dodge Viper. Like the Cobra, the Viper is an incredibly fast car. With twin racing stripes, the car looks like it just arrived from the racetrack!

The Viper's huge engine has ten **cylinders** and was originally designed for trucks. The Italian carmaker Lamborghini has also used this engine and has given it even more power.

At first, the Viper was available only in red or yellow. The GTS model, however, comes in many different colors, all with stripes.

ISTJ

Did You Know?

The Viper GTS has had two entries in the *Guinness Book of World Records*. One record, in 1998, was for towing a mobile home the fastest. The other record, in 1999, was for the fastest run by a blind driver!

FACTS AND STATS

First Model Year:
1996

Origin:
United States

Weight:
2,851 pounds
(1,293 kg)

Engine:
7,990 cc V10, front-mounted

Maximum Power:
378 hp

Acceleration:
0 to 60 miles (0 to 97 km) per hour in 4.5 seconds

Maximum Speed:
177 miles (285 km) per hour

The powerful GTS can be a challenge to drive fast, even on dry roads. If it rains, you might want to leave the Viper at home!

FERRARI F50

For decades, the Italian carmaker Ferrari has been world famous for its fast and beautiful sports cars. The company created the amazing F50 to celebrate its fiftieth anniversary. Ferrari built only 349 F50s. The F50's engine was originally used in **Formula One** racing cars.

The body, doors, and seats of the F50 are made of lightweight carbon fiber.

Most of the space in the back of the F50 is needed for the big V12 engine. Four exhaust pipes stick out through holes in the bumper.

FACTS AND STATS

First Model Year:
1996

Origin:
Italy

Weight:
2,712 pounds
(1,230 kg)

Engine: 4,699 cc V12,
mid-mounted

Maximum Power:
520 hp

Acceleration:
0 to 60 miles (0 to 97 km)
per hour in 3.7 seconds

Maximum Speed:
202 miles (325 km) per hour

The F50 accelerates to 100 miles (161 km) per hour in 8 seconds and 150 miles (241 km) per hour in 18 seconds.

Did You Know?

Although the F50 is a very expensive car, you still have to roll the windows up and down by hand!

JAGUAR XJ220S

The British carmaker Jaguar has built many exciting sports cars. In the late 1980s, Jaguar designed a **supercar** called the XJ220. The company delivered the first XJ220 in 1992. Two years later, Jaguar produced an even faster version called the XJ220S.

Did You Know?

In 1994, racing driver Martin Brundle reached 217 miles (349 km) per hour in an XJ220S. At the time, this speed was the fastest ever recorded for a road car.

The XJ220S is one of the widest sports cars ever made. An enormous **spoiler** at the back of the XJ220S keeps the car stable at high speeds.

The XJ220S was built by Tom Walkinshaw Racing (TWR). TWR based its design on a racing car — the Jaguar XJ220C.

The XJ220S has a carbon fiber body that is even lighter than the XJ220's aluminum body. The car has twin **turbochargers** and produces almost 700 hp — over 100 hp more than the XJ220.

LAMBORGHINI MURCIÉLAGO

Ferrucio Lamborghini was a tractor maker from northern Italy. Unhappy with the Ferrari he owned, he decided he could build a better car himself. In 1966, his company began making the Muira, a supercar with a V12 engine mounted sideways behind the seats. The Murciélago is Lamborghini's tenth model.

The roof and doors of the Murciélago are made of steel. The rest of the car is made of carbon fiber.

Did You Know?

The **emblem** on the hood of a Lamborghini has a figure of a charging bull. The bull is a symbol of both beauty and power.

It is hard to see behind you in the Murciélago. The best way to back up the car is to open the door and look over your shoulder!

The Murciélago is easier to drive than previous Lamborghinis. It has **four-wheel drive** and a safety system that slows down the car if it starts to lose its grip on the road.

McLAREN F1

McLaren is famous for creating very successful racing cars. In 1993, the British firm began selling a road car called the F1. The ultimate supercar, the F1 was the fastest road car ever and the first car to cost one million dollars.

Did You Know?

A yearly service at the garage for the F1 costs about $40,000!

A huge BMW engine takes up most of the space in the back of the F1. From a standstill, the car can reach 100 miles (161 km) per hour in just over 6 seconds.

The F1 has a driver's seat in the middle. The two passenger seats are located slightly behind it.

McLaren built a hundred F1 road cars before the company stopped making them in 1998. Each F1 took nearly two months to build.

MERCEDES-BENZ SL500

The German carmaker Mercedes-Benz is famous for its luxury **sedans,** but it also makes exciting sports cars. The SL500 is a high-performance car with many special features — including a hard top that folds into the trunk.

Did You Know?

The seat cushion of an SL500 has a built-in massager!

The SL500 has a satellite navigation system, a stereo system, and a video screen that are all voice-activated.

At the click of a button,
the SL500's hard top folds
down into the trunk in just
17 seconds.

FACTS AND STATS

First Model Year:
2001

Origin:
Germany

Weight:
3,900 pounds
(1,770 kg)

Engine:
4,966 cc V8, front-mounted

Maximum Power:
302 hp

Acceleration:
0 to 60 miles (0 to 97 km)
per hour in 6.3 seconds

Maximum Speed:
155 miles (249 km) per hour

The SL500 is
the latest in a
long line of sporty cars
from Mercedes-Benz with the "SL"
name. This 1956 190SL was driven
by Elvis Presley in the movie *GI Blues*.

PAGANI ZONDA C12 S

Although the Pagani Zonda is built in Italy, it was designed by Horacio Pagani, who is from Argentina. This amazing car is named after a wind that blows from the Andes Mountains in Argentina. The Zonda is the newest and most exclusive supercar. Only thirty Zondas were built in the first year.

Did You Know?

When you buy a Pagani Zonda, you get your own pair of special, handmade driving shoes.

The Zonda has no trunk at all! The only luggage space is behind the seats.

The back of the Zonda C12S contains an enormous V12 engine from Mercedes-Benz.

FACTS AND STATS

First Model Year:
2001

Origin:
Italy

Weight:
2,756 pounds (1,250 kg)

Engine:
7,010 cc V12, mid-mounted

Maximum Power:
562 hp

Acceleration:
0 to 60 miles (0 to 97 km) per hour in 3.7 seconds

Maximum Speed:
220 miles (354 km) per hour

The Zonda might remind you of a fighter plane. The car has a glass roof and twin spoilers, and its exhaust pipes look like the back end of a jet engine.

PORSCHE 911 GT2

The German company Porsche has been making the 911 model since the 1960s. In 2001, Porsche began selling the ultimate 911 — the GT2. With a **rollbar**, heavy-duty brakes, and an incredibly powerful engine, the GT2 is more like a racing car than a road car. It is actually the fastest road car Porsche has ever built.

Did You Know?

Porsche claims the GT2 can accelerate to 186 miles (300 km) per hour and then brake to a stop in less than 60 seconds.

The GT2's **flat-6 engine** is located in the back of the car, behind the rear wheels. With its twin turbos, this engine produces a tremendous amount of horsepower.

The GT2's rear wing and side panels have vents to cool the huge engine. The car also has vents in front to cool the **radiator** and brakes.

FACTS AND STATS

First Model Year:
2001

Origin:
Germany

Weight:
3,175 pounds (1,440 kg)

Engine:
3,600 cc turbo flat-6,
rear-mounted

Maximum Power: 455 hp

Acceleration:
0 to 60 miles (0 to 97 km)
per hour in 4.1 seconds

Maximum Speed:
197 miles (317 km) per hour

The GT2 is 10 percent more powerful and 7 percent lighter than an ordinary 911 Turbo.

TVR TUSCAN

The British firm TVR has been making affordable sports cars for over forty years. In 2000, the company began selling the Tuscan. TVR made the car as light as possible and gave it a powerful **inline-6 engine**. The Tuscan is extremely fast but costs much less than other cars with similar performance.

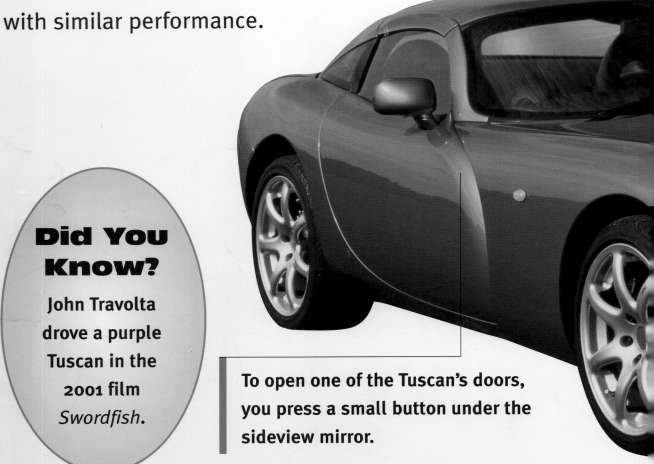

Did You Know?

John Travolta drove a purple Tuscan in the 2001 film *Swordfish*.

To open one of the Tuscan's doors, you press a small button under the sideview mirror.

The Tuscan's roof and rear window can be removed and stored in the car's large trunk. There is even enough space left over for a couple of suitcases!

The Tuscan's big engine takes up most of the space under the hood. It powers the car to 180 miles (290 km) per hour.

GLOSSARY

aluminum: a lightweight metal that is often used in the construction of cars.

carbon fiber: a threadlike material that is light and very strong.

convertible: a car with a top that can be folded down.

cylinders: can-shaped spaces in an engine where fuel explodes to create power.

emblem: on a car, a figure or design that identifies the carmaker.

fiberglass: a light, strong material made of glass fibers and plastic.

flat-6 engine: an engine with six cylinders arranged horizontally, or "flat," so that two rows of three cylinders are facing each other.

Formula One: an auto racing series that features extremely fast cars on tracks with many twists and turns.

four-wheel drive: a system used on some cars that delivers power from the engine to all four wheels.

gears: toothed wheels in a car's transmission that are turned by the engine. Gears of different sizes allow a car to be driven at different speeds without the engine spinning too quickly or too slowly.

horsepower: a unit of measurement for an engine's power that was originally based on the pulling strength of a horse.

inline-6 engine: an engine with six cylinders arranged vertically in a row.

radiator: a piece of equipment that keeps an engine from getting too hot by cooling the liquid that flows around the cylinders.

retro: having a style from the past.

rollbar: a metal framework inside a car that keeps a person from getting crushed if the car rolls over.

satellite navigation system: a system that uses information from satellites to help a driver find a route to any destination.

sedans: passenger cars that usually have hard tops that cannot be removed, seating for four or more people, and either two or four doors.

sensors: devices on a car that can detect something, such as low tire pressure or darkness.

spoiler: an attachment on a car's body that uses the force of flowing air to keep the car firmly on the ground at high speeds.

supercar: a very expensive sports car that has incredible performance and is usually built in small numbers.

turbochargers: devices that force extra air into an engine's cylinders to increase horsepower.

V8 engine: an engine that has eight cylinders arranged in a "V" shape, with four cylinders on each side.

V12 engine: an engine that has twelve cylinders arranged in a "V" shape, with six cylinders on each side.

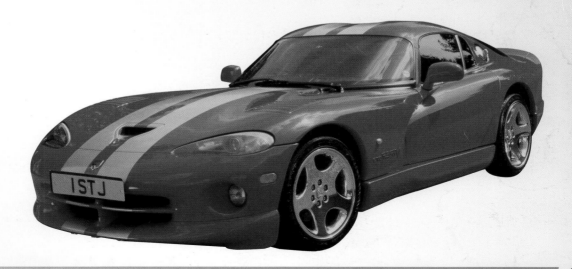

INDEX